GREAT AMERICAN
BRAND NAME
RECIPES COOKBOOK

Publications International, Ltd.

Louis Weber, C.E.O.
Publications International, Ltd.
7373 North Cicero Avenue
Lincolnwood, Illinois 60646

Permission is never granted for commercial purposes.

Printed and bound in Yugoslavia.

h g f e d c b a

ISBN 0-88176-591-0

Library of Congress Catalog Card Number: 89-60929

MINUTE® is a registered trademark of General Foods Corporation.

Pictured on the front cover: Top row, left to right—Northwest Cheesecake Supreme
(page 306), Rainbow Fruit Salad *(page 75)*, Cheese-Stuffed Beef Rolls *(page 194)*. Middle
row, left to right—Ginger Pineapple Mold *(page 73)*, Marinated Kabobs *(page 134)*,
Marinated Shrimp & Vegetables *(page 90)*. Bottom row, left to right—Marinated Beef
Salad *(page 85)*, Crème de Cacao Torte *(page 359)*, Broccoli and Pasta *(page 218)*.

Pictured on the back cover: Top row, left to right—Fresh Vegetable Salad *(page 64)*,
New Orleans Crumb Cake *(page 350)*, Garden Chicken Salad *(page 84)*. Middle row, left to
right—Ham Pasta Primavera *(page 204)*, Cool and Creamy Cucumber Spread *(page 11)*,
Caribbean Fudge Pie *(page 325)*. Bottom row, left to right—Fluffy Grasshopper Pie *(page
327)* Golden Gate Grill *(page 243)*, Shantung Chicken *(page 149)*.

CONTENTS

Your Guide to Great Cooking

GREAT AMERICAN BRAND NAME RECIPES COOKBOOK is just that—a great collection of recipes developed and tested by the great American food companies, using their brand-name products. Expert home economists at top American food companies have developed, tested, and written these recipes to help you use their products. We have selected the most popular recipes for this book, many of which have been collected from the pages of our best-selling FAVORITE RECIPES™ Magazine. Now you have a convenient volume containing all of your favorites.

The variety of these recipes is apparent as you glance through the book. You'll find recipes for any occasion. We've included appetizers, beverages, soups and salads, main dishes of all kinds, breads and rolls, and a variety of desserts. From breakfast to supper and even midnight snacks, there are recipes for any time of day. For busy days, you'll find terrific recipes that get you out of the kitchen in a hurry. When you have time to be creative, choose one of the gourmet specialties. Recipes with the international flair of Italy, the Orient, Mexico, and France are included, along with home-style dishes that represent American cooking from every region. You can try new ideas for family meals, or present something elegant for a special occasion.

When looking through this book, you'll notice that a large number of these recipes can be prepared in your microwave oven. Some have been developed especially for microwave cooking. Although these recipes have been thoroughly tested, the microwave cooking times given must be considered approximate. Higher-wattage microwave ovens cook foods more quickly than those with low wattage. In addition, the starting temperature of the food, the shape and size of the pieces, and the food's depth in the cooking utensil can affect cooking time. Most recipes will give a test for doneness. It's best to use the cooking times in the recipe as a guideline; check to see if the food is done before adding more time.

Some recipes in this book are followed by a nutritional analysis, giving numeric values for the number of calories and amount of protein, fat, carbohydrate, sodium, and cholesterol in each serving of the recipe. This information is based on the ingredients listed in the recipe. For cases in which a choice of ingredients is given, the first option was used in computing the nutritional analysis. If the ingredient list calls for "2 tablespoons butter or margarine," for example, the nutritional information applies to the recipe made with butter, not margarine. Ingredients listed as "optional" or "if desired" were not included in the analysis. If a range of servings is given in the recipe, the analysis was computed for the largest number of servings. Please remember that, just as individual foods of the same type are different, their nutrition content can vary. Consequently, these figures should be viewed as approximations.

As wonderful as these recipes are, you'll also find that this book is appealing to browse through. You'll get great ideas for menu-planning by looking at the large full-color photographs throughout the book. And with a collection of recipes this comprehensive, you'll always have just the right recipe at your fingertips. So start cooking—and enjoy the delicious results!

APPETIZERS

Good friends and good times call for these tempting appetizers. Look for easy dips and spreads to welcome impromptu guests, elegant first courses to set the tone for an important meal, and wonderful party fare for gatherings large and small. You'll find a variety of sensational starters to let your hospitality shine.

Cracked Black Pepper and Herb Spread

- **1 package (8 ounces) cream cheese, softened**
- **6 ounces goat cheese (Montrachet, Chèvre or feta)**
- **¼ cup WISH-BONE® Italian Dressing**
- **½ cup chopped red onion**
- **1 teaspoon fresh chopped thyme leaves***
- **1 teaspoon fresh chopped sage leaves****
- **1 teaspoon cracked black pepper**

In food processor or blender, process all ingredients until blended; cover and chill. Garnish, if desired, with additional cracked black pepper and serve with assorted fresh vegetables, crackers and breads.
Makes about 2 cups spread.
   ***Substitution:** Use ½ teaspoon dried thyme leaves.
   ****Substitution:** Use ½ teaspoon dried sage leaves.
   Note: Also terrific with Wish-Bone® Robusto Italian, Herbal Italian Blended Italian, Lite Italian or Lite Classic Dijon Vinaigrette Dressing.

Curried Peanut Dip

- **1 pouch CAMPBELL'S® Onion Soup and Recipe Mix**
- **1 cup sour cream**
- **1 cup plain yogurt**
- **¼ cup creamy peanut butter**
- **2 teaspoons curry powder**
  Chopped peanuts for garnish
  Fresh pear slices for garnish

1. In medium bowl, blend soup mix, sour cream, yogurt, peanut butter and curry powder. Cover; chill until serving time, at least 2 hours.
2. Garnish with chopped peanuts and pear slices. Serve with vegetable or fruit dippers.
Makes 2¼ cups.

Colorful Carrot Dip

- **1 8-ounce package *Light* PHILADELPHIA BRAND Neufchâtel Cheese, softened**
- **½ cup finely shredded carrot**
- **1 teaspoon parsley flakes**
- **⅛ teaspoon salt**
  Dash of pepper

Combine neufchâtel cheese, carrots and seasonings, mixing until well blended. Chill. Serve with vegetable dippers.
1 cup.
   Variations: Substitute freeze-dried chopped chives for parsley flakes.
   Substitute ½ teaspoon dried basil leaves, crushed, for parsley flakes.
   Substitute ¼ teaspoon dill weed or lemon pepper for parsley flakes.

Bacon-Horseradish Dip

- **1 pouch CAMPBELL'S® Onion Soup and Recipe Mix**
- **2 cups sour cream**
- **5 slices bacon, cooked and crumbled**
- **1 tablespoon prepared horseradish**
- **1 teaspoon Dijon-style mustard**
  Cooked bacon curl for garnish

1. In medium bowl, combine soup mix, sour cream, crumbled bacon, horseradish and mustard; mix well. Cover; chill until serving time, at least 2 hours.
2. Garnish with bacon curl. Serve with chips or crackers.
Makes 2 cups.

Colorful Carrot Dip

Baked Cream Cheese Appetizer

**1 4-ounce package refrigerated
    crescent dinner rolls
1 8-ounce package
    PHILADELPHIA BRAND
    Cream Cheese
½ teaspoon dill weed
1 egg yolk, beaten**

Unroll dough on lightly floured surface; press together seams to form 12×4-inch rectangle. Sprinkle top of cream cheese with half of dill; lightly press dill into cream cheese. Place cream cheese, dill-side down, in center of dough. Sprinkle cream cheese with remaining dill. Enclose cream cheese in dough by bringing sides of dough together, pressing edges to seal. Place on lightly greased cookie sheet; brush with egg yolk. Bake at 350°, 15 to 18 minutes or until lightly browned. Serve with assorted crackers and apple slices.
8 servings.

Variations: Substitute combined ½ teaspoon dried rosemary leaves, crushed, and ½ teaspoon paprika for dill weed.

Substitute *Light* PHILADELPHIA BRAND Neufchâtel Cheese for Cream Cheese.

Baked Cream Cheese Appetizer

Blue Cheese Walnut Spread

**1 envelope KNOX® Unflavored
    Gelatine
¾ cup cold water
½ cup sour cream
⅓ cup milk
1 tablespoon lemon juice
1 teaspoon Worcestershire
    sauce
4 ounces blue cheese, crumbled
1 package (8 ounces) cream
    cheese, softened
½ cup walnuts**

In small saucepan, sprinkle unflavored gelatine over ¼ cup cold water; let stand 1 minute. Stir over low heat until gelatine is completely dissolved, about 3 minutes.

In blender, process sour cream, remaining ½ cup water, milk, lemon juice, Worcestershire sauce and cheeses until blended. While processing, through feed cap, gradually add gelatine mixture, then walnuts; process until blended. Pour into 7½×3¾×2¼-inch loaf pan or 4-cup bowl; chill until firm, about 3 hours. Unmold onto lettuce-lined platter and serve, if desired, with crackers, party-size breads and fruits.
Makes about 3¾ cups spread.

Eggplant Caviar

**1 large eggplant, unpeeled
¼ cup chopped onion
2 tablespoons lemon juice
1 tablespoon olive or vegetable
    oil
1 small clove garlic
½ teaspoon salt
¼ teaspoon TABASCO® pepper
    sauce
    Sieved egg white (optional)
    Lemon slice (optional)**

Preheat oven to 350°F. Place eggplant in shallow baking dish. Bake 1 hour or until soft, turning once. Trim off ends; slice eggplant in half lengthwise. Place cut-side-down in colander and let drain 10 minutes. Scoop out pulp; reserve pulp and peel. In blender or food processor combine eggplant peel, onion, lemon juice, oil, garlic, salt and Tabasco® sauce. Cover; process until peel is finely chopped. Add eggplant pulp. Cover; process just until chopped. Place in serving dish. Garnish with egg white and lemon slice, if desired. Serve with toast points.
Makes about 1½ cups.

Garlic Spread

**1 8-ounce package
    PHILADELPHIA BRAND
    Cream Cheese, softened
½ cup PARKAY Margarine,
    softened
2 tablespoons chopped parsley
2 tablespoons chopped onion
1 garlic clove, minced**

Combine cream cheese and margarine, mixing until well blended. Add remaining ingredients; mix well. Chill.
Approximately 1⅔ cups.

Chili con Queso

2 tablespoons CRISCO® Oil
¼ cup minced onion
1 can (7½ ounces) whole tomatoes, drained and finely chopped
1 can (4 ounces) chopped green chilies, undrained
¼ teaspoon salt
2 cups shredded Cheddar or Monterey Jack cheese (about 8 ounces)
⅓ cup whipping cream
Nacho chips

Heat Crisco® Oil in 1-quart saucepan. Add onion. Cook over medium-high heat, stirring occasionally, until onion is tender. Add tomatoes, chilies and salt. Stir to blend and break apart tomatoes. Heat to boiling. Reduce heat to medium-low. Cook, stirring occasionally, 15 minutes. Remove from heat. Stir in cheese and cream. Cook over low heat, stirring constantly, until cheese melts. Serve with nacho chips.
About 1¾ cups.

Variation: Hot Chili con Queso. Follow recipe above, substituting jalapeño peppers (drained) for green chilies.

Toasted Sesame Cheese Spread

2 tablespoons KIKKOMAN Soy Sauce
1 package (3 oz.) cream cheese
4 teaspoons sesame seed, toasted
Assorted crackers

Pour soy sauce over cream cheese block in small dish, turning over several times to coat all sides. Cover; refrigerate 2 hours, turning cheese block over often. Remove cheese block from soy sauce and roll in sesame seed. Refrigerate until ready to serve with crackers.
Makes 4 to 6 appetizer servings.

Creamy Chili Dip

2 packages (8 ounces each) cream cheese or reduced-calorie cream cheese, softened
¾ cup V8® Vegetable Juice
1 can (4 ounces) chopped chilies
½ cup VLASIC® or EARLY CALIFORNIA® Chopped Pitted Ripe Olives
½ cup chopped sweet red pepper
2 teaspoons grated onion
¼ teaspoon hot pepper sauce
Fresh cilantro for garnish

1. In medium bowl with mixer at medium speed, beat cream cheese until smooth and fluffy.
2. Gradually beat in V8 juice until smooth and thoroughly blended.
3. Stir in chilies, olives, red pepper, onion and hot pepper sauce. Cover; refrigerate until serving time, at least 4 hours.
4. Garnish with fresh cilantro. Serve with fresh vegetables or chips for dipping.
Makes 4 cups.

Per tablespoon: 28 calories, 0 g protein, 3 g fat, 1 g carbohydrate, 50 mg sodium, 8 mg cholesterol.

Vegetable Dip Verde

1 cup cottage cheese
1 cup firmly packed parsley sprigs
½ cup chopped green onions
⅓ cup capers, drained
2 hard-cooked eggs, peeled, quartered
2 cloves garlic
1 tablespoon lemon juice
¼ teaspoon salt
¼ teaspoon TABASCO® pepper sauce

In container of blender or food processor combine all ingredients. Cover; process until smooth. Remove to serving bowl. Cover; refrigerate at least 1 hour. Serve with cut-up fresh vegetables.
Makes about 1½ cups.

Tropical Fruit Dip

½ cup mayonnaise
¼ cup sour cream
3 tablespoons lime juice
1 teaspoon honey
½ teaspoon ground cumin
¼ teaspoon TABASCO® pepper sauce
½ cup shredded coconut

In medium bowl combine mayonnaise, sour cream, lime juice, honey, cumin and Tabasco® sauce; mix well. Stir in coconut. Cover, refrigerate at least 1 hour. Serve with cut-up fresh fruit.
Makes about 1 cup.

Manhattan Clam Dip

1 (3-ounce) package cream cheese, softened
¼ cup mayonnaise or salad dressing
1 (8-ounce) container BORDEN® or MEADOW GOLD® Sour Cream
½ cup BENNETT'S® Cocktail Sauce
1 or 2 (6½-ounce) cans SNOW'S® or DOXSEE® Minced Clams, drained
2 tablespoons chopped green onion
1 teaspoon REALEMON® Lemon Juice from Concentrate

In small mixer bowl, beat cheese and mayonnaise until smooth. Stir in remaining ingredients. Chill. Garnish as desired. Serve with assorted fresh vegetables or WISE® COTTAGE FRIES® Potato Chips. Refrigerate leftovers.
Makes about 2 cups.

Manhattan Clam Dip

Chicken with Oriental Dipping Sauce

Chicken with Oriental Dipping Sauce

2 packages (12 ounces each)
SWANSON® Frozen Fried
Plump & Juicy® Chicken
Dipsters® or 1 package
(28 ounces) SWANSON®
Frozen Fried Chicken
Nibbles®
¾ cup V8® Vegetable Juice
¼ cup packed light brown sugar
2 tablespoons rice vinegar or
dry sherry
1 tablespoon soy sauce
1 tablespoon cornstarch
¼ teaspoon grated fresh ginger

To Microwave:
1. Prepare chicken dipsters according to package directions.
2. In medium microwave-safe bowl, stir together remaining ingredients. Cover with waxed paper; microwave on HIGH 3 minutes or until hot and bubbling, stirring once during cooking. Serve chicken with sauce for dipping.
Makes 1 cup sauce.
   Note: This sauce is also great to use for dipping MRS. PAUL'S® fish sticks, fried eggplant, zucchini sticks and onion rings.

Chicken Liver Pâté

2 packages (8 ounces each)
SWANSON® Frozen Chicken
Livers
¼ cup water
1 pouch CAMBPELL'S® Onion
Soup and Recipe Mix
2 slices bacon, chopped
¼ cup butter or margarine, cut
up
2 tablespoons brandy
½ teaspoon dry mustard
¼ teaspoon dried thyme leaves,
crushed
¼ teaspoon pepper
Fresh parsley for garnish
Chopped hard-cooked egg for
garnish

To Microwave:
1. Remove frozen livers from boxes but do not remove from pouches. Place in 2-quart microwave-safe casserole. Microwave, uncovered, at 50% power 5 minutes, turning pouches over once during cooking. Let stand 5 minutes. Remove livers from pouches and place in same casserole.

Eggplant Spread

¼ cup olive oil
1 medium eggplant, peeled and
coarsely chopped (about
1 pound)
½ cup chopped onion
1 clove garlic, minced
¾ cup V8® Vegetable Juice
¼ cup toasted chopped pine nuts
2 tablespoons chopped fresh
parsley
2 teaspoons soy sauce
1 teaspoon sugar
⅛ teaspoon pepper
Pita bread wedges

1. In 10-inch skillet over medium heat, in hot oil, cook eggplant, onion and garlic about 15 minutes or until eggplant is tender, stirring often.
2. In covered blender or food processor, blend eggplant mixture until smooth.
3. In medium bowl, combine eggplant mixture, V8 juice, pine nuts, parsley, soy sauce, sugar and pepper. Stir until thoroughly mixed. Cover; refrigerate until serving time, at least 2 hours. Serve with pita bread wedges.
Makes 3 cups.

Per tablespoon: 18 calories, 0 g protein, 2 g fat, 1 g carbohydrate, 28 mg sodium, 0 mg cholesterol.

Quick Paté Mold

½ pound liverwurst, cut into
small pieces
1 (8-ounce) package cream
cheese, softened
2 tablespoons finely chopped
onion
1 teaspoon WYLER'S® or
STEERO® Chicken-Flavor
Instant Bouillon
Parsley, optional
Melba rounds

In small mixer bowl, combine liverwurst, cheese, onion and bouillon; beat until smooth. Turn into well-oiled 2-cup mold. Chill. Unmold; garnish with parsley if desired. Serve with Melba rounds. Refrigerate leftovers.
Makes 1 appetizer mold.

2. Add water, soup mix and bacon. Cover with lid; microwave on HIGH 5 minutes, stirring twice during cooking. Reduce power to 50%. Cover; microwave 4 minutes or until livers are no longer pink, stirring once during cooking.

3. In covered blender or food processor, combine liver mixture, butter, brandy, mustard, thyme and pepper. Blend until smooth.

4. Spoon mixture into 3-cup crock. Cover; refrigerate 4 hours or overnight. Garnish with parsley and egg. Serve with crackers.
Makes about 3 cups.

Guacamole

**3 ripe medium avocados, seeded and peeled
2 tablespoons REALIME® Lime Juice from Concentrate *or* REALEMON® Lemon Juice from Concentrate
1/2 teaspoon garlic salt
1/2 teaspoon sugar
1/4 teaspoon pepper**

In blender container or food processor, mash avocados. Add remaining ingredients; mix well. Chill to blend flavors. Garnish as desired. Serve with WISE® BRAVOS® or LA FAMOUS® Tortilla Chips or fresh vegetables. Refrigerate leftovers.
Makes about 2 cups.

Variations: Add 1 or more of the following: sour cream, cooked crumbled bacon, chopped water chestnuts, chopped fresh tomato, chopped chilies.

Cool and Creamy Cucumber Spread

**3 medium cucumbers
1 (8-ounce) *plus* 1 (3-ounce) package cream cheese, softened
1/2 cup sour cream
1/4 cup snipped fresh dill*
1 1/2 teaspoons lemon juice
1 envelope LIPTON® Vegetable Recipe Soup Mix**

Thinly slice 1 cucumber and arrange in bottom of lightly oiled 4-cup ring mold; set aside.

Peel, seed and coarsely chop remaining cucumbers. With food processor or electric mixer, combine cream cheese, 1 cup chopped cucumber, sour cream, dill, lemon juice and vegetable recipe soup mix until smooth. Stir in remaining chopped cucumber. Turn into prepared mold; chill until firm, at least 3 hours. To serve, unmold onto serving platter and fill center, if desired, with cherry tomatoes and leaf lettuce. Serve with assorted crackers.
Makes about 3 1/2 cups spread.

Substitution: Use 2 tablespoons dried dill weed.

Molded Cheese

**2 packages (4-serving size) or 1 package (8-serving size) JELL-O® Brand Orange or Lemon Flavor Gelatin
1 1/2 cups boiling water
1/2 pound (2 1/2 cups) finely grated sharp Cheddar cheese**

**1 package (8 ounces) cream cheese, softened
1 cup (1/2 pint) sour cream
1/2 cup chopped scallions
1/4 cup chopped parsley
3 tablespoons prepared horseradish
1 tablespoon Worcestershire sauce**

Dissolve gelatin in boiling water. Combine remaining ingredients in large bowl; with electric mixer at medium speed, beat until well blended. Gradually blend into gelatin. Pour into 6-cup mold. Chill until firm, about 3 hours. Unmold. Garnish with fresh fruit or vegetables, if desired. Serve as an appetizer with assorted crackers.
Makes 5 1/2 cups or 11 servings.

Cool and Creamy Cucumber Spread

Garden Vegetable Spread

    1 8-ounce container Soft
       PHILADELPHIA BRAND
       Cream Cheese
    ½ cup shredded carrot
    ½ cup shredded zucchini
    1 tablespoon chopped parsley
    ¼ teaspoon garlic salt
       Dash of pepper

Combine ingredients; mix well. Chill. Serve with party rye or pumpernickel bread slices or assorted crackers. *1⅓ cups.*

Variation: Serve with LENDER'S Pre-Sliced Frozen Plain Bagelettes, toasted.

Florentine Dip

    1 8-ounce package *Light*
       PHILADELPHIA BRAND
       Neufchâtel Cheese, softened
    ½ cup plain yogurt
    2 tablespoons milk
    1 10-ounce package frozen
       spinach, thawed, well-
       drained, chopped
    2 hard-cooked eggs, finely
       chopped
    ¼ teaspoon pepper
    ¼ teaspoon salt

Combine neufchâtel cheese, yogurt and milk, mixing until well blended. Stir in remaining ingredients. Serve with vegetable dippers. *2½ cups.*

Florentine Dip

Hearty Herbed Cheese Spread

    1 pouch CAMPBELL'S® Onion
       Soup and Recipe Mix
    2 packages (8 ounces each)
       cream cheese, softened
    2 cups shredded sharp Cheddar
       cheese (8 ounces), at room
       temperature
    ½ cup chopped fresh parsley
    2 tablespoons milk
    1 teaspoon dried basil leaves,
       crushed
    1 teaspoon dried tarragon
       leaves, crushed
    ½ teaspoon dried dill weed,
       crushed
    2 tablespoons cracked pepper
       Paprika for garnish

1. In medium bowl, combine soup mix, cheeses, parsley, milk, basil, tarragon and dill; beat with wooden spoon until well blended.
2. Line 9-inch pie plate with plastic wrap, letting wrap hang over edge. Spoon cheese mixture into pie plate, packing down firmly. Cover; chill until serving time, at least 4 hours.
3. Invert pie plate over serving dish and remove pie plate and plastic from cheese. Smooth surface of cheese with a knife to remove any wrinkles. Press cracked pepper into sides of cheese; sprinkle top with paprika. Serve with crackers.
Makes 3¼ cups.

Note: To make a fancy design on cheese spread, first cut a piece of cardboard into desired shape (flower, Christmas tree, etc.), and lay cardboard on cheese spread. Sprinkle paprika around design. Carefully remove cardboard to leave a stenciled design in paprika.

Warm Herb Cheese Spread

    3 (8-ounce) packages cream
       cheese, softened
    ¼ cup BORDEN® or MEADOW
       GOLD® Milk
    ¼ cup REALEMON® Lemon Juice
       from Concentrate
    ½ teaspoon *each* basil, oregano,
       marjoram and thyme leaves
    ¼ teaspoon garlic powder
    ½ pound cooked shrimp,
       chopped (1½ cups), optional

Preheat oven to 350°. In large mixer bowl, beat cheese until smooth. Gradually beat in milk then ReaLemon® brand. Stir in remaining ingredients. Pour into 9-inch quiche dish or pie plate. Cover; bake 15 minutes or until hot. Garnish as desired. Serve warm with crackers or fresh vegetables. Refrigerate leftovers.
Makes about 4 cups.

Microwave: In 9-inch pie plate, prepare cheese spread as above. Cook on 50% power (medium) 5 to 6 minutes or until hot. Stir before serving.

Hot Crabmeat Appetizer

    1 8-ounce package
       PHILADELPHIA BRAND
       Cream Cheese, softened
    1 7½-ounce can crabmeat,
       drained, flaked
    2 tablespoons finely chopped
       onion
    2 tablespoons milk
    ½ teaspoon KRAFT Cream Style
       Horseradish
    ¼ teaspoon salt
       Dash of pepper
    ⅓ cup sliced almonds, toasted

Combine all ingredients except almonds, mixing until well blended. Spoon mixture into 9-inch pie plate; sprinkle with almonds. Bake at 375°, 15 minutes. Serve with crackers. *Approximately 1½ cups.*

Variations: Substitute 8-ounce can minced clams, drained, for crabmeat.

Omit almonds; sprinkle with dill weed.

Hot Beef Dip

- ¼ cup chopped onion
- 1 tablespoon PARKAY Margarine
- 1 cup milk
- 1 8-ounce package PHILADELPHIA BRAND Cream Cheese, cubed
- 1 3-ounce package smoked sliced beef, chopped
- 1 4-ounce can mushrooms, drained
- ¼ cup (1 ounce) KRAFT Grated Parmesan Cheese
- 2 tablespoons chopped parsley

Saute onions in margarine. Add milk and cream cheese; stir over low heat until cream cheese is melted. Add remaining ingredients; heat thoroughly, stirring occasionally. Serve hot with French bread slices, if desired.
2½ cups.

Variation: Substitute 2½-ounce package smoked sliced turkey for 3-ounce package smoked sliced beef.

Serving Suggestion: For a colorful variety, serve with French, whole-wheat or rye bread cubes.

Hot Artichoke Dip

- 1 package (9 ounces) frozen artichoke hearts, thawed
- ½ pint (8 ounces) sour cream
- ¼ cup grated Parmesan cheese
- 1 envelope LIPTON® Golden Onion Recipe Soup Mix
- Buttered bread crumbs
- Suggested Dippers*

Preheat oven to 350°

In food processor or blender, puree artichokes. Add sour cream and cheese; process until smooth. Stir in golden onion recipe soup mix. Turn into 2½-cup casserole, then top with bread crumbs. Bake uncovered 30 minutes or until heated through. Serve with Suggested Dippers.
Makes about 2¼ cups dip.

***Suggested Dippers:** Use carrot or celery sticks, whole mushrooms or sliced zucchini.

Microwave Directions: Omit bread crumbs. Prepare mixture as above. Heat at HIGH (Full Power), turning casserole occasionally, 8 minutes or until heated through. Let stand covered 5 minutes. Serve as above.

Mexican-Style Appetizer

Mexican-Style Appetizer

- 1 can (11½ ounces) CAMPBELL'S® Condensed Bean with Bacon Soup
- 1 package (1¼ ounces) taco seasoning mix
- ¼ teaspoon hot pepper sauce
- 1 cup sour cream
- 1 can (4 ounces) chopped green chilies, drained
- ½ cup VLASIC® or EARLY CALIFORNIA® Sliced Pimento-Stuffed Olives
- 1 cup shredded longhorn cheese (4 ounces)
- ½ cup alfalfa sprouts
- ½ cup chopped CAMPBELL'S FRESH® Tomato
- Tortilla chips

1. In small bowl, combine soup, taco seasoning mix and hot pepper sauce; stir until blended. On large serving plate, spread mixture into a 6-inch round. Spread sides and top of bean mixture with sour cream to cover.

2. Layer chilies, olives, cheese, alfalfa sprouts and tomato over sour cream. Cover; refrigerate until serving time, at least 4 hours. Surround with tortilla chips.
Makes 10 appetizer servings.

Layered Crab Spread

- 2 (8-ounce) packages cream cheese, softened
- 2 tablespoons REALEMON® Lemon Juice from Concentrate
- 1 teaspoon Worcestershire sauce
- ¼ teaspoon garlic powder
- 2 tablespoons finely chopped green onion
- ¾ cup BENNETT'S® Chili Sauce
- 1 (6-ounce) can ORLEANS® White Crab Meat, drained

In large mixer bowl, beat cheese, ReaLemon® brand, Worcestershire and garlic powder until fluffy; stir in onion. Spread evenly on 10-inch plate. Top with chili sauce then crabmeat. Cover; chill thoroughly. Garnish as desired. Serve with assorted crackers. Refrigerate leftovers.
Makes 10 to 12 servings.

Nutty Blue Cheese Vegetable Dip

Party Cheese Ball

- 2 8-ounce packages PHILADELPHIA BRAND Cream Cheese, softened
- 2 cups (8 ounces) shredded CRACKER BARREL Brand Sharp Natural Cheddar Cheese
- 1 tablespoon chopped pimento
- 1 tablespoon chopped green pepper
- 1 tablespoon finely chopped onion
- 2 teaspoons worcestershire sauce
- 1 teaspoon lemon juice
  Dash of ground red pepper
  Dash of salt
  Chopped pecans

Combine cream cheese and cheddar cheese, mixing at medium speed on electric mixer until well blended. Add all remaining ingredients except pecans; mix well. Chill several hours. Shape into ball; roll in pecans. Serve with crackers.
Approximately 2 cups.
Variation: Omit pecans. Roll in finely chopped parsley, dried beef or toasted chopped almonds.

Nutty Blue Cheese Vegetable Dip

- 1 cup mayonnaise or salad dressing
- 1 (8-ounce) container BORDEN® or MEADOW GOLD® Sour Cream
- ¼ cup (1 ounce) crumbled blue cheese
- 1 tablespoon finely chopped onion
- 2 teaspoons WYLER'S® or STEERO® Beef-Flavor Instant Bouillon
- ½ to ¾ cup coarsely chopped walnuts
  Assorted fresh vegetables

In medium bowl, combine mayonnaise, sour cream, blue cheese, onion and bouillon; mix well. Stir in nuts; cover and chill. Stir before serving. Garnish as desired. Serve with vegetables. Refrigerate leftovers.
Makes about 2 cups.

Pine Nut Cheese Spread

- 1 8-ounce package PHILADELPHIA BRAND Cream Cheese, softened
- 2 tablespoons KRAFT Grated Parmesan Cheese
- ¼ cup chopped green pepper
- 1 tablespoon finely chopped onion
- 2 teaspoons chopped pimento
  Dash of ground red pepper
- ⅓ cup pine nuts or slivered almonds, toasted

Combine all ingredients except pine nuts, mixing until well blended. Chill. Shape into log. Coat with pine nuts just before serving.
1 cup.
Variation: Substitute *Light* PHILADELPHIA BRAND Neufchâtel Cheese for Cream Cheese. Increase Parmesan cheese to ¼ cup (1 ounce). Spoon into serving container. Top with pine nuts just before serving.
Hint: Homemade cheese spreads in colorful containers make great hostess gifts. Include the recipe for an added personal touch.

Savory Cheddar Spread

- 1 8-ounce package PHILADELPHIA BRAND Cream Cheese, softened
- ½ cup MIRACLE WHIP Salad Dressing
- 1 cup (4 ounces) 100% Natural KRAFT Shredded Mild Cheddar Cheese
- 2 tablespoons green onion slices
- 8 crisply cooked bacon slices, crumbled
- ½ cup crushed buttery crackers

Combine cream cheese and salad dressing, mixing until well blended. Add cheddar cheese and onions; mix well. Spoon into 9-inch pie plate; sprinkle with combined bacon and crumbs. Bake at 350°, 15 minutes. Serve with additional crackers.
2 cups.

Variation: Substitute ¼ cup bacon flavored bits for crumbled bacon.

Microwave: Microwave cream cheese on Medium (50%) 30 seconds. Assemble recipe as directed except for sprinkling with bacon and crumbs. Microwave on High 4 minutes or until thoroughly heated, turning dish every 2 minutes. Sprinkle with combined bacon and crumbs. Serve as directed.

Refreshing Cucumber Dip

- 1 8-ounce package PHILADELPHIA BRAND Cream Cheese, softened
- ½ cup sour cream
- 1 tablespoon milk
- 1 teaspoon grated onion
- ¼ teaspoon worcestershire sauce
- ⅓ cup finely chopped cucumber

Combine all ingredients except cucumbers, mixing until well blended. Stir in cucumbers. Chill several hours or overnight. Serve with chips or vegetable dippers.
1⅔ cups.

Pineapple-Almond Cheese Spread

- 2 cans (8 ounces each) DOLE® Crushed Pineapple
- 1 package (8 ounces) cream cheese, softened
- 4 cups shredded sharp Cheddar cheese
- ½ cup mayonnaise
- 1 tablespoon soy sauce
- 1 cup DOLE™ Chopped Natural Almonds, toasted
- ½ cup finely chopped DOLE™ Green Bell Pepper
- ¼ cup minced green onion or chives
- DOLE™ Celery stalks or assorted breads

Drain pineapple. In large bowl, beat cream cheese until smooth; beat in Cheddar cheese, mayonnaise and soy sauce until smooth. Stir in pineapple, almonds, green pepper and onion. Refrigerate, covered. Use to stuff celery stalks or serve as dip with assorted breads. Serve at room temperature.
Makes 4 cups.

Hawaiian Coconut Spread

- 1 8-ounce container Soft PHILADELPHIA BRAND Cream Cheese
- 2 tablespoons KRAFT Apricot, Pineapple or Peach Preserves
- ⅓ cup flaked coconut

Combine cream cheese and preserves, mixing until well blended. Add coconut; mix well. Chill. Serve with nut bread slices.
1⅓ cups.

Variations: Add ⅛ teaspoon anise seed.

Substitute ¼ cup whole berry cranberry sauce for KRAFT Preserves.

Zucchini Chive Dip

- 1 8-ounce container Soft PHILADELPHIA BRAND Cream Cheese
- 3 tablespoons milk
- 1 small zucchini, shredded
- 3 tablespoons chopped chives
- ⅛ teaspoon salt

Combine cream cheese and milk, mixing until well blended. Add remaining ingredients; mix well. Chill. Serve with vegetable dippers or chips.
1 cup.

Quick Mexican Spread

- 1 8-ounce package *Light* PHILADELPHIA BRAND Neufchâtel Cheese, softened
- 1 4-ounce can chopped green chilies, drained

Combine neufchâtel cheese and chilies, mixing until well blended. Chill. Serve with tortilla chips or spread over warm tortillas or corn bread.
1 cup.

Piña Pepper Spread

- 1 can (8 ounces) DOLE® Crushed Pineapple, drained
- ½ cup bottled taco sauce
- 1 package (8 ounces) cream cheese, softened
- Taco chips or crackers

Combine pineapple and taco sauce in small bowl. Place cream cheese on serving plate in block or cut into individual servings. Spoon pineapple mixture over top. Serve with taco chips or crackers.
Makes 4 servings.

Piña Pepper Spread

Peppy Bean Dip

- **1 pouch CAMPBELL'S® Onion Soup and Recipe Mix**
- **½ cup sour cream**
- **1 can (16 ounces) refried beans**
- **½ cup salsa**
- **1 large clove garlic, minced VLASIC® or EARLY CALIFORNIA® Sliced Pitted Ripe Olives for garnish**

1. In medium bowl, combine soup mix, sour cream, beans, salsa and garlic; mix well. Cover; chill until serving time, at least 2 hours.
2. Garnish with olives. Serve with corn chips or vegetable dippers.
Makes 2½ cups.

Mustard Sauce

- **2 tablespoons CRISCO® Oil**
- **2 tablespoons all-purpose flour**
- **2 tablespoons dry mustard**
- **½ teaspoon salt**
- **1 cup milk**

Blend Crisco® Oil, flour, mustard and salt in small saucepan. Cook over medium-high heat 1 minute. Stir in milk. Cook, stirring constantly, until sauce thickens and bubbles.
About 1 cup.

Roasted Red Pepper Mousse Spread

- **1 envelope KNOX® Unflavored Gelatine**
- **½ cup cold water**
- **2 cups (1 pint) whipping or heavy cream**
- **1 jar (8 ounces) roasted red peppers, drained and coarsely chopped**
- **½ cup mayonnaise**
- **1 cup loosely packed basil leaves***
- **¼ cup grated Parmesan cheese**
- **1 small clove garlic, finely chopped**
- **½ teaspoon salt**
- **⅛ teaspoon pepper**

In small saucepan, sprinkle unflavored gelatine over cold water; let stand 1 minute. Stir over low heat until gelatine is completely dissolved, about 3 minutes. Remove from heat and let stand until lukewarm, about 2 minutes.

In large bowl, with electric mixer, beat cream until soft peaks form. Gradually add red peppers, mayonnaise, basil, cheese, garlic, salt and pepper. While beating, gradually add lukewarm gelatine mixture and beat until blended. Pour into 7-cup mold or bowl; chill until firm, about 3 hours. Unmold and serve, if desired, with sliced Italian bread, toasted.
Makes about 6 cups spread.
***Substitution:** Use 1 cup chopped fresh parsley plus 1 teaspoon dried basil leaves.

Shrimp Spread

- **2 (8-ounce) packages cream cheese, softened**
- **½ cup REALEMON® Lemon Juice from Concentrate**
- **2 (4¼-ounce) cans ORLEANS® Shrimp, drained and soaked as label directs**
- **1 to 2 tablespoons finely chopped green onion**
- **1 tablespoon prepared horseradish**
- **1 teaspoon Worcestershire sauce**
- **¼ teaspoon pepper**
- **⅛ teaspoon garlic powder**

In small mixer bowl, beat cheese until fluffy; gradually beat in ReaLemon® brand. Stir in remaining ingredients. Chill to blend flavors. Garnish as desired. Serve with crackers or fresh vegetables. Refrigerate leftovers.
Makes about 3 cups.

Salmon Mousse

- **2 envelopes KNOX® Unflavored Gelatine**
- **1 can (15½ ounces) salmon, drained (reserve liquid)***
- **1 stalk celery, cut into 3-inch pieces**
- **1 small onion, quartered**
- **½ medium cucumber, peeled, seeded and quartered**
- **1 cup (½ pint) whipping or heavy cream**
- **¾ cup mayonnaise**
- **¼ cup lemon juice**
- **1 teaspoon dried dill weed**
- **½ teaspoon salt (optional)**

In medium saucepan, sprinkle unflavored gelatine over reserved salmon liquid blended with enough water to equal 1 cup; let stand 1 minute. Stir over low heat until gelatine is completely dissolved, about 5 minutes.

In blender or food processor, process gelatine mixture, vegetables, cream, mayonnaise and lemon juice until blended. Add salmon, dill and salt; process until blended. Pour into 6-cup mold or bowl; chill until firm, about 3 hours. Unmold and serve with assorted crackers.
Makes about 5½ cups spread.
***Substitution:** Use 2 cans (6½ ounces each) tuna, drained (reserve liquid).

Shrimp Spread

Spicy Appetizer Dip

- 1 (8-ounce) can crushed pineapple in its own juice
- 1 cup COLLEGE INN® Chicken or Beef Broth
- 3 tablespoons cornstarch
- 2 tablespoons soy sauce
- 2 tablespoons white wine vinegar
- 2 tablespoons firmly packed light brown sugar
- ¼ teaspoon crushed red pepper
Cocktail franks, ham cubes or fresh vegetables

Drain pineapple, reserving juice. In small saucepan, blend reserved juice, broth, cornstarch, soy sauce, vinegar, brown sugar and red pepper. Cook and stir until mixture thickens and boils. Stir in pineapple. Serve hot or cold with cocktail franks, ham cubes or vegetables.
Makes 2 cups.

Mini Monte Cristo Sandwiches

- 2 tablespoons butter or margarine, softened
- 2 tablespoons prepared mustard
- 8 slices white bread
- 4 slices fontina or Swiss cheese (about 4 ounces)
- 4 slices cooked ham (about 4 ounces)
- 3 eggs
- ½ cup milk
- 1 envelope LIPTON® Golden Onion Recipe Soup Mix
- ¼ cup butter or margarine

Blend 2 tablespoons butter with mustard; evenly spread on each bread slice. Equally top 4 bread slices with cheese and ham; top with remaining bread, buttered side down. Cut each sandwich into 4 triangles.

Beat eggs, milk and golden onion recipe soup mix until well blended. Dip sandwiches in egg mixture, coating well.

In large skillet, melt ¼ cup butter and cook sandwiches over medium heat, turning once, until golden.
Makes about 16 mini sandwiches.

Spicy Appetizer Dip

Country Pâté

- 4 slices bacon
- 1 pound ground beef
- ½ pound cooked ham, cut into ¼-inch pieces
- ½ pound raw skinless boneless chicken breast, cut into ¼-inch pieces
- 2 eggs
- 1 pouch CAMPBELL'S® Onion Soup and Recipe Mix
- 2 tablespoons brandy
- ½ teaspoon pepper
- ¼ teaspoon ground nutmeg
Watercress for garnish
Cherry tomatoes for garnish

To Microwave:
1. Arrange bacon slices ½ inch apart across bottom and up sides of 9- by 5-inch microwave-safe loaf dish; set aside.

2. In medium bowl, thoroughly mix beef, ham, chicken, eggs, soup mix, brandy, pepper and nutmeg. Spoon meat mixture into bacon-lined dish, packing down firmly. Fold ends of bacon over filling.

3. Cover with waxed paper; microwave on HIGH 8 minutes, rotating once during cooking. Carefully pour off fat. Cover; microwave on HIGH 8 minutes or until center is firm, rotating dish twice during cooking. Let stand, covered, 10 minutes. Pour off fat. Invert onto serving plate. Cover; refrigerate until serving time, at least 4 hours.

4. Cut loaf into thin slices. Garnish with watercress and cherry tomatoes. Serve with crackers and mustard.
Makes 18 appetizer servings.

Note: If you are using a temperature probe, cook pâté to an internal temperature of 175° to 185°F.

Herbed Cheese Pinwheel Canapes

    1 8-ounce package
       PHILADELPHIA BRAND
       Cream Cheese, softened
    2 tablespoons chopped parsley
    2 teaspoons lemon juice
  ½ teaspoon dried basil leaves,
       crushed
  ⅛ teaspoon pepper
  ⅛ teaspoon garlic powder
    1 1-pound unsliced whole-wheat
       bread loaf, crusts trimmed
       Soft PARKAY Margarine
  ¼ cup finely chopped pecans
  ¼ cup sesame seed
    1 tablespoon worcestershire
       sauce

Herbed Cheese Pinwheel Canapes

Combine cream cheese, parsley, juice and seasonings, mixing until well blended. Slice bread lengthwise into ½-inch slices. Roll each slice to ¼-inch thickness. Evenly spread each bread slice with cream cheese mixture; roll up, starting at narrow end. Spread bread rolls with margarine, excluding ends. In small skillet, combine remaining ingredients; cook 3 minutes or until worcestershire sauce evaporates. Cool. Coat bread rolls with pecan mixture. Cover; chill at least 30 minutes. Cut each bread roll crosswise into ½-inch slices.
Approximately 2½ dozen.

Cheese & Nut Stuffed Bread Slices

    1 loaf Italian or French bread
       (about 16 inches long)
    1 (8-ounce) *plus* 1 (3-ounce)
       package cream cheese,
       softened
    4 tablespoons butter or
       margarine, softened
    1 cup shredded Cheddar cheese
       (about 4 ounces)
    1 envelope LIPTON® Vegetable
       Recipe Soup Mix
  ½ cup chopped walnuts

Trim ends of bread, then cut bread crosswise into 4 pieces. Hollow out center of each piece, leaving ½-inch shell; reserve shells (save bread for fresh bread crumbs).

With food processor or electric mixer, combine cream cheese with butter until smooth. Add Cheddar cheese, vegetable recipe soup mix and walnuts; process until blended. Pack into reserved shells. Wrap in plastic wrap or wax paper, then chill at least 4 hours. To serve, cut into ½-inch slices.
Makes about 2 dozen slices.

  Note: Store any remaining cheese mixture, covered, in refrigerator and serve as a spread with crackers.

Mexican Shrimp Cocktail

  ½ cup WISH-BONE® Italian
       Dressing
  ½ cup chopped tomato
    1 can (4 ounces) chopped green
       chilies, undrained
  ¼ cup chopped green onions
1½ teaspoons honey
  ¼ teaspoon hot pepper sauce
    1 pound medium shrimp,
       cleaned and cooked
    2 teaspoons finely chopped
       coriander (cilantro) or
       parsley

In medium bowl, combine Italian dressing, tomato, chilies, green onions, honey and hot pepper sauce. Stir in shrimp. Cover and marinate in refrigerator, stirring occasionally, at least 2 hours. Just before serving, stir in coriander.
Makes about 6 servings.

  Note: Also terrific with Wish-Bone® Robusto Italian, Lite Italian, Blended Italian or Herbal Italian Dressing.

Cheese Stuffed Tomatoes

    1 cup BORDEN® or MEADOW
       GOLD® Cottage Cheese
  ¼ cup (1 ounce) crumbled blue
       cheese
    1 teaspoon celery seed
    1 teaspoon prepared mustard
  ¼ teaspoon onion powder
  30 cherry tomatoes, tops
       removed and seeded

In medium bowl, combine cheeses and seasonings; mix well. Spoon cheese mixture into tomatoes; cover and chill. Refrigerate leftovers.
Makes 30 appetizers.

Cheesy Potato Skins

    4 large baking potatoes, baked
      Oil
 ¼ lb. VELVEETA Pasteurized
      Process Cheese Spread,
      cubed
    2 tablespoons chopped red or
      green pepper
    2 crisply cooked bacon slices,
      crumbled
    1 tablespoon green onion slices
      Sour cream

Cut potatoes in half lengthwise; scoop out centers, leaving ¼-inch shell. Fry shells, a few at a time, in deep hot oil, 375°, 2 to 3 minutes or until golden brown; drain. Place on cookie sheet. Top with process cheese spread; broil until process cheese spread begins to melt. Top with remaining ingredients.
8 appetizers.

Preparation time: 60 minutes
Cooking time: 10 minutes

Beer Batter Fried Veggies 'n Things

      Oil
    1 envelope LIPTON® Golden
      Onion Recipe Soup Mix
    1 cup all-purpose flour
    1 teaspoon baking powder
    2 eggs
 ½ cup beer
    1 tablespoon prepared mustard
      Suggested Veggies 'n Things*

In deep-fat fryer, heat oil to 375°.
   Meanwhile, in large bowl, beat golden onion recipe soup mix, flour, baking powder, eggs, beer and mustard until smooth and well blended. Let batter stand 10 minutes. Dip Suggested Veggies 'n Things into batter, then carefully drop into hot oil. Fry, turning once, until golden brown; drain on paper towels. Serve warm.
Makes about 4 cups veggies 'n things.
   Suggested Veggies 'n Things:
Use any of the following to equal 4 to 5 cups—broccoli florets, cauliflowerets, sliced mushrooms or zucchini, or chilled mozzarella sticks.

Herb Appetizer Cheesecake

    1 cup dry bread crumbs
 ¼ cup PARKAY Margarine,
      melted
 ¼ cup olive oil
    2 cups fresh basil leaves
 ½ teaspoon salt
    1 garlic clove, cut in half
    2 8-ounce packages
      PHILADELPHIA BRAND
      Cream Cheese, softened
    1 cup ricotta cheese
    3 eggs
 ½ cup (2 ounces) KRAFT Grated
      Parmesan Cheese
 ½ cup pine nuts

Combine crumbs and margarine; press onto bottom of 9-inch springform pan. Bake at 350°, 10 minutes.
   Place oil, basil, salt and garlic in blender container. Cover; process on high speed until smooth. Combine basil mixture, cream cheese and ricotta cheese, mixing at medium speed on electric mixer until well blended. Add eggs, one at a time, mixing well after each addition. Blend in parmesan cheese; pour over crust. Top with pine nuts. Bake at 325°, 1 hour and 15 minutes. Loosen cake from rim of pan; cool before removing rim of pan. Serve warm or at room temperature.

Garnish with tomato rose and fresh basil, if desired. Chill any remaining cheesecake.
16 servings.
   Variation: Substitute 1 cup chopped parsley and 1 tablespoon dried basil leaves for fresh basil leaves.

Beef Kushisashi

 ½ cup KIKKOMAN Soy Sauce
 ¼ cup chopped green onions
      and tops
    2 tablespoons sugar
    1 tablespoon vegetable oil
 1½ teaspoons cornstarch
    1 clove garlic, pressed
    1 teaspoon grated fresh ginger
      root
 2½ pounds boneless beef sirloin
      steak

Blend soy sauce, green onions, sugar, oil, cornstarch, garlic and ginger in small saucepan. Simmer, stirring constantly, until thickened, about 1 minute; cool. Cover and set aside. Slice beef into ⅛-inch-thick strips about 4 inches long and 1 inch wide. Thread onto bamboo or metal skewers keeping meat as flat as possible; brush both sides of beef with sauce. Place skewers on rack of broiler pan; broil to desired degree of doneness.
Makes 10 to 12 appetizer servings.

Beef Kushisashi

Baked Stuffed Shrimp

Baked Stuffed Shrimp

**1 pound jumbo raw shrimp
(about 12 to 16), peeled,
leaving tails on**
1 cup chopped mushrooms
1/3 cup chopped onion
1 clove garlic, finely chopped
**1 teaspoon WYLER'S® or
STEERO® Chicken-Flavor
Instant Bouillon**
1/4 cup margarine or butter
**1 1/2 cups soft bread crumbs
(3 slices bread)**
**1 tablespoon chopped pimiento
Melted margarine or butter
Chopped parsley, optional**

Preheat oven to 400°. In large skillet, cook mushrooms, onion, garlic and bouillon in margarine until tender. Remove from heat; stir in crumbs and pimiento. Cut a slit along underside of each shrimp; do not cut through. Remove vein; brush entire shrimp with margarine. Mound stuffing mixture in hollow of each shrimp. Place in greased shallow baking dish. Bake 10 to 12 minutes or until hot. Garnish with parsley if desired. Refrigerate leftovers.
Makes 6 to 8 servings.
Microwave: In 1-quart glass measure, microwave margarine on full power (high) 45 seconds or until melted. Add mushrooms, onion, garlic and bouillon. Microwave on full power (high) 3 minutes or until onion is tender. Stir in crumbs and pimiento. Prepare shrimp as above. Place in 2 greased 12×7-inch shallow baking dishes or 1 (12-inch) round glass platter. Microwave on full power (high) 3 minutes or until hot. Proceed as above.

Baked Stuffed Clams

**12 clams, well scrubbed*
Water**
**1 envelope LIPTON® Vegetable
Recipe Soup Mix**
2 cups fresh bread crumbs
1 teaspoon oregano
1/8 teaspoon pepper
2 tablespoons oil
**2 tablespoons grated Parmesan
cheese**

In large skillet, arrange clams, then add 1/2 inch water. Cook covered over medium-high heat 5 minutes or until clams open. Remove clams, reserving 3/4 cup liquid; strain liquid. (Discard any unopened clams.) Remove clams from shells, then chop clams; reserve 12 shell halves.
Preheat oven to 350°. In small bowl, combine vegetable recipe soup mix, bread crumbs, oregano and pepper. Stir in clams and reserved liquid. Stuff reserved shells with clam mixture. Arrange on baking sheet; drizzle with oil, then sprinkle with cheese. Bake 15 minutes or until golden.
Makes 12 stuffed clams.
***Substitution:** Use 2 cans (6 1/2 ounces each) minced or chopped clams, drained (reserve 1/4 cup liquid). Mix reserved liquid with 1/2 cup water. Shells can be purchased separately.
Microwave Directions: Omit oil. Cook and stuff clams as above. On plate, arrange clams and heat uncovered at HIGH (Full Power) 5 minutes or until heated through, rearranging clams once.

Baked Artichoke Squares

3 tablespoons CRISCO® Oil
**1 cup chopped fresh
mushrooms**
1/4 cup thinly sliced celery
1 clove garlic, minced
**1 can (14 ounces) artichoke
hearts, drained and chopped**
1/3 cup chopped green onion
**1/2 teaspoon dried marjoram
leaves**
1/4 teaspoon dried oregano leaves
1/4 teaspoon cayenne
**1 cup shredded Cheddar cheese
(about 4 ounces)**
**1 cup shredded Monterey Jack
cheese (about 4 ounces)**
2 eggs, slightly beaten
Pastry:
1 1/2 cups all-purpose flour
1/2 teaspoon salt
1/2 cup CRISCO® Oil
1/4 cup milk

Preheat oven to 350°F. Heat Crisco® Oil in medium skillet. Add mushrooms, celery and garlic. Sauté until celery is tender. Remove from heat. Stir in artichoke hearts, onion, marjoram, oregano and cayenne. Add Cheddar cheese, Monterey Jack cheese and eggs. Mix well. Set aside.
For pastry, combine flour and salt in medium mixing bowl. Blend Crisco® Oil and milk in small mixing bowl. Add to flour mixture. Stir with fork until mixture forms a ball. Press dough in bottom and 1 1/2 inches up sides of 13×9-inch pan. Bake at 350°F, 10 minutes.
Spread cheese mixture on baked crust. Bake at 350°F, about 20 minutes, or until center is set. Cool slightly. Cut into 24 squares. Serve warm.
2 dozen appetizers.

Appetizer Ham Logs

    2 cups ground ham
    1 egg, beaten
 1/4 teaspoon pepper
 1/4 cup seasoned fine dry bread
        crumbs
 1/2 cup horseradish sauce
    1 tablespoon prepared mustard
 1/8 teaspoon celery salt
      Vegetable oil for frying
      Pimiento strips

Combine ham, egg and pepper in medium bowl; mix well. Shape into 1-
inch logs or balls. Roll in bread
crumbs. Refrigerate, covered, 1 hour.

To make mustard sauce, combine
horseradish sauce, mustard and celery salt in small bowl until well
blended. Refrigerate, covered, until
serving time.

Heat 3 inches oil in heavy, large
saucepan over medium-high heat until oil is 365°F; adjust heat to main-
tain temperature. Fry ham logs, a few
at a time, 2 to 3 minutes or until
golden. Drain on paper towels. Garnish with pimiento strips. Serve with
mustard sauce.
Makes about 24 appetizers.

Favorite recipe from **National Pork Producers Council**

Ham-Wrapped Oysters

    3 tablespoons prepared
        horseradish
 1/2 pound ham, cut into
        3×1×1/4-inch strips
    2 dozen fresh oysters, shucked
    3 tablespoons butter or
        margarine, melted
    1 tablespoon lemon juice
 1/4 teaspoon garlic powder

Spread horseradish on 1 side of each
ham strip. Place 1 oyster on each ham
strip; roll up and secure with wooden
pick. Arrange on broiler pan. Combine butter, lemon juice and garlic
powder in small cup. Brush each ham
roll with some of the lemon-butter.
Broil, 5 inches from heat, 10 to 15
minutes or until edges of oysters curl,
brushing occasionally with the remaining lemon-butter.
Makes 24 appetizers.

Favorite recipe from **National Pork Producers Council**

**Top: Appetizer Ham Logs, Miniature Teriyaki Pork Kabobs (page 23);
bottom: Ham-Wrapped Oysters, Rumaki (page 22)**

Buffalo-Style Chicken Wings

Oil
12 chicken wings (about 2 pounds)
½ cup all-purpose flour
2 tablespoons butter or margarine
¼ cup sliced green onions
1 medium clove garlic, finely chopped
1 cup (8 ounces) WISH-BONE® Sweet 'n Spicy® French Dressing
1 teaspoon thyme leaves
1 teaspoon oregano leaves
1 teaspoon ground cumin
½ teaspoon hot pepper sauce* WISH-BONE® Chunky Blue Cheese Dressing Celery sticks

In deep-fat fryer or large heavy skillet, heat oil to 375°.

Cut tips off chicken wings (save tips for soup). Halve chicken wings at joint. Lightly coat chicken with flour, then carefully drop chicken, a few pieces at a time, into hot oil. Fry, turning occasionally, 15 minutes or until golden brown; drain on paper towels.

Meanwhile, in large skillet, melt butter and cook green onions with garlic over medium heat, stirring occasionally, 3 minutes or until onions are tender. Remove from heat and stir in sweet 'n spicy French dressing, thyme, oregano, cumin and hot pepper sauce. Add chicken and toss to coat. Serve with chunky blue cheese dressing and celery sticks.
Makes 24 appetizers.

*Variations: First Alarm Chicken Wings: Add 1 teaspoon hot pepper sauce.

Second Alarm Chicken Wings: Add 1½ teaspoons hot pepper sauce.

Third Alarm Chicken Wings: Add 2 teaspoons hot pepper sauce.

Note: Also terrific with Wish-Bone® Lite Sweet 'n Spicy French, Russian or Lite Russian Dressing.

Marinated Mushrooms

½ cup WISH-BONE® Italian & Cheese Dressing
2 pounds fresh mushrooms
2 teaspoons lemon juice

In large saucepan, heat Italian & cheese dressing and cook mushrooms over medium heat, stirring occasionally, 5 minutes. Add lemon juice. Remove mushrooms with dressing to large shallow baking dish. Cover and marinate in refrigerator, stirring occasionally, 4 hours or overnight.
Makes about 4 cups mushrooms.

Note: Also terrific with Wish-Bone® Italian, Robusto Italian, or Lite Italian Dressing.

Marinated Antipasto

1½ pounds medium raw shrimp, peeled, deveined and cooked
6 ounces Provolone cheese, cut into cubes
1 (6-ounce) can pitted ripe olives, drained
½ cup sliced green onions
1 cup vegetable oil
⅔ cup REALEMON® Lemon Juice from Concentrate
2 tablespoons Dijon-style mustard
2 teaspoons sugar
1½ teaspoons thyme leaves
1 teaspoon salt
4 ounces Genoa salami, cut into cubes
1 large red pepper, seeded and cut into squares

Place shrimp, cheese, olives and onions in large shallow dish. In small bowl or jar, combine remaining ingredients except salami and pepper; mix well. Pour over shrimp mixture.

Cover; refrigerate 6 hours or overnight, stirring occasionally. Add salami and pepper; toss. Drain; serve with toothpicks. Refrigerate leftovers.
Makes about 8 cups.

Rumaki

16 slices bacon
1 pound chicken livers, cut into quarters
1 can (8 ounces) sliced water chestnuts, drained
⅓ cup soy sauce
2 tablespoons packed brown sugar
1 tablespoon Dijon-style mustard

Cut bacon slices in half crosswise. Wrap ½ slice bacon around piece of chicken liver and water chestnut slice. Secure with wooden pick. (Reserve any remaining water chestnut slices for another use.) Arrange on broiler pan. Combine soy sauce, brown sugar and mustard in small bowl. Brush over bacon rolls. Broil, 6 inches from heat, 15 to 20 minutes or until bacon is crisp and chicken livers are done, turning and brushing with soy sauce mixture occasionally.
Makes about 32 appetizers.

*Favorite recipe from **National Pork Producers Council***

Marinated Antipasto

Chicken Wings with Honey & Orange Sauce

- **12 chicken wings (about 2 pounds)**
- **1 envelope LIPTON® Golden Onion Recipe Soup Mix**
- **⅓ cup honey**
- **¼ cup water**
- **¼ cup frozen concentrated orange juice, partially thawed and undiluted**
- **¼ cup sherry**
- **1 tablespoon prepared mustard**
- **2 teaspoons soy sauce**
- **¼ teaspoon ground ginger**
- **3 dashes hot pepper sauce**

Preheat oven to 350°.

Cut tips off chicken wings (save tips for soup). Halve remaining chicken wings at joint.

In 13×9-inch baking dish, blend remaining ingredients; add chicken and turn to coat. Bake uncovered, basting occasionally, 40 minutes or until chicken is done and sauce is thickened.
Makes 24 appetizers.

Microwave Directions: In 13×9-inch baking dish, prepare chicken wings and sauce as above. Heat uncovered at HIGH (Full Power), basting and rearranging chicken occasionally, 20 minutes or until chicken is done and sauce is thickened. Let stand uncovered 5 minutes.

Chicken Wings with Honey & Orange Sauce

done, turning and basting with sauce occasionally.
Makes about 24 appetizers.

*Favorite recipe from **National Pork Producers Council***

Miniature Teriyaki Pork Kabobs

- **1 pound boneless pork, cut into 4×1×½-inch strips**
- **1 can (11 ounces) mandarin oranges**
- **1 small green bell pepper, cut into 1×¼×¼-inch strips**
- **¼ cup teriyaki sauce**
- **1 tablespoon honey**
- **1 tablespoon vinegar**
- **⅛ teaspoon garlic powder**

Soak 24 (8-inch) bamboo skewers in water 10 minutes. Thread pork strips accordion-style with mandarin oranges on skewers. Place 1 pepper strip on end of each skewer. Arrange on broiler pan.

For sauce, combine teriyaki sauce, honey, vinegar and garlic powder in small bowl; mix well. Brush sauce over kabobs. Broil, 6 inches from heat, about 15 minutes or until pork is

Thai Chicken Strips

- **½ cup WISH-BONE® Italian Dressing**
- **¼ cup dry white wine**
- **1 tablespoon sugar**
- **1 tablespoon soy sauce**
- **1 tablespoon finely chopped coriander (cilantro) or parsley**
- **½ teaspoon ground ginger**
- **½ teaspoon ground cumin**
- **¼ teaspoon paprika**
- **¼ cup sesame seeds, well toasted**
- **1½ pounds boneless chicken breasts, cut into lengthwise strips**

In food processor or blender, process Italian dressing, wine, sugar, soy sauce, coriander, ginger, cumin and paprika until blended. In large shallow baking dish, combine dressing mixture, sesame seeds and chicken. Cover and marinate in refrigerator, stirring occasionally, at least 3 hours.

Remove chicken and marinade to large shallow baking pan or aluminum foil-lined broiler rack. Broil chicken with marinade, turning occasionally, 10 minutes or until done. Garnish as desired.
Makes about 20 appetizers.

Note: Also terrific with Wish-Bone® Robusto Italian, Classic Dijon Vinaigrette, Herbal Italian, Lite Italian, Blended Italian or Lite Classic Dijon Vinaigrette Dressing.

Filled New Potatoes

- **2 pounds (18) small new potatoes**
- **1 8-ounce container Soft PHILADELPHIA BRAND Cream Cheese**
- **Caviar**
- **Chopped chives**

Cook potatoes in boiling salted water 15 to 20 minutes or until tender; drain. Cut thin slice from bottom to form base; scoop out top with melon ball cutter. Fill with cream cheese; top with caviar or chives. Serve warm.
1½ dozen.

Golden Mini Quiches

1 envelope LIPTON® Golden
    Onion Recipe Soup Mix
1½ cups light cream or half and
    half
3 eggs, beaten
    Pastry for double-crust pie*
1 cup shredded Swiss cheese
    (about 4 ounces)

Preheat oven to 400°.

In medium bowl, thoroughly blend golden onion recipe soup mix, cream and eggs; set aside.

On lightly floured board, roll pastry ⅛ inch thick; cut into 36 (2½-inch) circles. Press into 7½×9¾-inch muffin pans. Evenly fill prepared pans with cheese, then egg mixture. Bake 25 minutes or until knife inserted in center comes out clean and pastry is golden. Serve warm.
Makes 3 dozen mini quiches.

Variation: For one 9-inch quiche, bake one 9-inch unbaked pastry shell at 375°, 10 minutes. Fill pastry shell with cheese, then egg mixture. Bake 40 minutes or until quiche tests done and pastry is golden.
Makes about 7 servings.

Freezing/Reheating Directions: Mini quiches can be baked, then frozen. Simply wrap in heavy-duty aluminum foil; freeze. To reheat, unwrap and bake at 350°, 15 minutes or until heated through. **OR,** place 12 quiches on plate and microwave at HIGH (Full Power) 4 minutes or until heated through, turning plate once.

Deviled Stuffed Eggs

12 hard-cooked eggs
⅓ cup finely chopped VLASIC®
    Country Classic Sweet
    Gherkins
⅓ cup MARIE'S® Refrigerated
    Buttermilk Spice Ranch
    Style Salad Dressing
2 tablespoons finely chopped
    onion
¼ teaspoon salt
    Finely chopped VLASIC®
    Country Classic Sweet
    Gherkins for garnish

1. Remove egg shells. Cut eggs in half lengthwise. Remove and chop egg yolks. Dice 1 egg white.
2. To make filling: In medium bowl, combine yolks, diced egg white, ⅓ cup gherkins, salad dressing, onion and salt.

3. Spoon about 1 tablespoon filling into each remaining egg white half. Cover; refrigerate until serving time, at least 4 hours.
4. To serve: Top each filled half with chopped gherkins.
Makes 22 appetizers.

Grilled Cheese

1 piece raclette cheese*
    (12 to 16 ounces)
1 tablespoon olive or vegetable
    oil
½ teaspoon ground oregano
    Sliced crusty French bread or
    large crackers

Place cheese in 10-inch iron skillet; brush with oil. Sprinkle oregano on top. Place bread slices around cheese in skillet.

Grill cheese, on covered grill, over medium-hot **KINGSFORD® Charcoal Briquets** 10 minutes or until cheese is very soft. Remove to table; spread cheese on bread slices.
Makes 6 servings.

*Raclette cheese is available at specialty cheese shops. You can try another soft cheese, such as Swiss, but cooking time may vary.

Crispy Fried Mushrooms

½ cup all-purpose flour
½ teaspoon salt
¼ teaspoon dry mustard
¼ teaspoon paprika
    Dash pepper
½ cup buttermilk
8 ounces whole fresh
    mushrooms
    CRISCO® Oil for frying

Mix flour, salt, mustard, paprika and pepper in large plastic food storage bag. Set aside. Place buttermilk in small bowl. Dip a few mushrooms at a time in buttermilk. Place in bag with flour mixture. Shake to coat.

Heat 2 to 3 inches Crisco® Oil in deep-fryer or heavy saucepan to 375°F. Fry a few mushrooms at a time, 2 to 3 minutes, or until deep golden brown, turning over several times. Drain on paper towels. Serve hot with *catsup*, if desired.
4 to 6 servings.

Crispy Fried Mushrooms

Spring Rolls

- ½ pound ground pork
- 1 teaspoon KIKKOMAN Soy Sauce
- 1 teaspoon dry sherry
- ½ teaspoon garlic salt
- 2 tablespoons vegetable oil
- 3 cups fresh bean sprouts
- ½ cup sliced onion
- 1 tablespoon KIKKOMAN Soy Sauce
- 1 tablespoon cornstarch
- ¾ cup water, divided
- 8 sheets egg roll skins
- ½ cup prepared biscuit mix
- 1 egg, beaten
  Vegetable oil for frying
  Hot mustard, tomato catsup and KIKKOMAN Soy Sauce

Combine pork, 1 teaspoon soy sauce, sherry and garlic salt; mix well. Let stand 15 minutes. Heat 2 tablespoons oil in hot wok or large skillet over medium-high heat; brown pork mixture in hot oil. Add bean sprouts, onion and 1 tablespoon soy sauce. Stir-fry until vegetables are tender-crisp; drain and cool. Dissolve cornstarch in ¼ cup water. Place about ⅓ cupful pork mixture on lower half of egg roll skin. Moisten left and right edges with cornstarch mixture. Fold bottom edge up to just cover filling. Fold left and right edges ½ inch over; roll up jelly-roll fashion. Moisten top edge with cornstarch mixture and seal. Complete all rolls. Combine biscuit mix, egg and remaining ½ cup water in small bowl; dip each roll in batter. Heat oil for frying in wok or large saucepan over medium-high heat to 370°F. Deep fry rolls, a few at a time, in hot oil 5 to 7 minutes, or until golden brown, turning often. Drain on paper towels. Slice each roll into 4 pieces. Serve with mustard, catsup and soy sauce as desired.
Makes 8 appetizer servings.

Grilled Oysters

- 12 to 16 fresh oysters in shells
- ½ cup butter or margarine
- 2 tablespoons lemon juice
- 2 tablespoons chopped parsley

Thoroughly scrub oysters. Arrange oysters on grill grid; do not open shells. Grill oysters, on uncovered grill, over medium-hot **KINGS-FORD® Charcoal Briquets** 12 to 15

"Philly" Stuffed Mushrooms

minutes or until shells steam open. (Discard any oysters that do not open.)

Meanwhile, in saucepan, combine butter, lemon juice and parsley. Heat butter mixture on edge of grill until butter is melted, stirring frequently.

Carefully remove cooked oysters from grill and serve hot with lemon-butter mixture spooned over.
Makes 4 appetizer servings.

Cantonese Meatballs

- 1 can (20 oz.) pineapple chunks in syrup
- 3 tablespoons brown sugar, packed
- 5 tablespoons KIKKOMAN Teriyaki Sauce, divided
- 1 tablespoon vinegar
- 1 tablespoon tomato catsup
- 1 pound lean ground beef
- 2 tablespoons instant minced onion
- 2 tablespoons cornstarch
- ¼ cup water

Drain pineapple; reserve syrup. Combine syrup, brown sugar, 3 tablespoons teriyaki sauce, vinegar and catsup; set aside. Mix beef with remaining 2 tablespoons teriyaki sauce and onion; shape into 20 meatballs. Brown meatballs in large skillet;

drain off excess fat. Pour syrup mixture over meatballs; simmer 10 minutes, stirring occasionally. Dissolve cornstarch in water; stir into skillet with pineapple. Cook and stir until sauce thickens and pineapple is heated through.
Makes 6 to 8 appetizer servings.

"Philly" Stuffed Mushrooms

- 2 pounds medium mushrooms
- 6 tablespoons PARKAY Margarine
- 1 8-ounce package PHILADELPHIA BRAND Cream Cheese, softened
- ½ cup (2 ounces) crumbled KRAFT Natural Blue Cheese
- 2 tablespoons chopped onion

Remove mushroom stems; chop enough stems to measure ½ cup. Cook half of mushroom caps in 3 tablespoons margarine over medium heat 5 minutes; drain. Repeat with remaining mushroom caps and margarine. Combine cream cheese and blue cheese, mixing until well blended. Stir in chopped stems and onions; fill mushroom caps. Place on cookie sheet; broil until golden brown.
Approximately 2½ dozen.

Cajun-Style Chicken Nuggets

- 1 envelope LIPTON® Onion or Onion-Mushroom Recipe Soup Mix
- 1/2 cup plain dry bread crumbs
- 1 1/2 teaspoons chili powder
- 1 teaspoon ground cumin
- 1 teaspoon thyme leaves
- 1/4 teaspoon red pepper
- 2 pounds boneless chicken breasts, cut into 1-inch pieces
  Oil

In large bowl, combine onion recipe soup mix, bread crumbs, chili powder, cumin, thyme and pepper. Dip chicken in bread crumb mixture, coating well.

In large skillet, heat 1/2 inch oil and cook chicken over medium heat, turning once, until done; drain on paper towels. Serve warm and, if desired, with assorted mustards.
Makes about 5 dozen nuggets.

Microwave Directions: Prepare chicken as above. In 13×9-inch baking dish, arrange chicken, then drizzle with 2 to 3 tablespoons oil. Heat uncovered at HIGH (Full Power) 6 minutes or until chicken is done, rearranging chicken once; drain on paper towels. Serve as above.

Curried Chicken Puffs

- 1/2 cup water
- 1/3 cup PARKAY Margarine
- 2/3 cup flour
  Dash of salt
- 2 eggs
- 1 8-ounce package PHILADELPHIA BRAND Cream Cheese, softened
- 1/4 cup milk
- 1/4 teaspoon salt
  Dash of curry powder
  Dash of pepper
- 1 1/2 cups chopped cooked chicken
- 1/3 cup slivered almonds, toasted
- 2 tablespoons green onion slices

Bring water and margarine to boil. Add flour and salt; stir vigorously over low heat until mixture forms ball. Remove from heat; add eggs, one at a time, beating until smooth after each addition. Place level measuring

Curried Chicken Puffs

tablespoonfuls of batter on ungreased cookie sheet. Bake at 400°, 25 minutes. Cool.

Combine cream cheese, milk, salt, curry powder and pepper, mixing until well blended. Add chicken, almonds and onions; mix lightly. Cut tops from cream puffs; fill with chicken mixture. Replace tops. Place puffs on cookie sheet. Bake at 375°, 5 minutes or until warm.
Approximately 1 1/2 dozen.

Note: Unfilled cream puffs can be prepared several weeks in advance and frozen. Place puffs on a jelly roll pan and wrap securely in plastic wrap.

Empress Chicken Wings

- 1 1/2 pounds chicken wings (about 8 wings)
- 3 tablespoons KIKKOMAN Soy Sauce
- 1 tablespoon dry sherry
- 1 tablespoon minced fresh ginger root
- 1 clove garlic, minced
- 2 tablespoons vegetable oil
- 1/4 to 1/3 cup cornstarch
- 2/3 cup water
- 2 green onions and tops, cut diagonally into thin slices
- 1 teaspoon slivered fresh ginger root

Disjoint chicken wings; discard tips (or save for stock). Combine soy sauce, sherry, minced ginger and garlic in large bowl; stir in chicken. Cover and refrigerate 1 hour, stirring occasionally. Remove chicken; reserve marinade. Heat oil in large skillet over medium heat. Lightly coat chicken pieces with cornstarch; add to skillet and brown slowly on all sides. Remove chicken; drain off fat. Stir water and reserved marinade into same skillet. Add chicken; sprinkle green onions and slivered ginger evenly over chicken. Cover and simmer 5 minutes, or until chicken is tender.
Makes 4 to 6 appetizer servings.

Mini Cocktail Meatballs

- 1 envelope LIPTON® Onion, Onion-Mushroom, Beefy Mushroom or Beefy Onion Recipe Soup Mix
- 1 pound ground beef
- 1/2 cup plain dry bread crumbs
- 1/4 cup dry red wine or water
- 2 eggs, slightly beaten

Preheat oven to 375°.

In medium bowl, combine all ingredients; shape into 1-inch meatballs.

In shallow baking pan, arrange meatballs and bake 18 minutes or until done. Serve, if desired, with assorted mustards or tomato sauce.
Makes about 4 dozen meatballs.